D1405240

one pot
recipes

SIMPLE RECIPES FOR
STUNNING MEALS

LINDA DOESER

This is a Parragon Book
First published in 2004

Parragon
Queen Street House
4 Queen Street
Bath BA1 1HE

Copyright © Parragon 2004

All rights reserved. No part of this publication may be reproduced, stored
in a retrieval system or transmitted, in any form or by any means, electronic, mechanical,
photocopying, recording or otherwise, without the prior
permission of the copyright holder.

Created and produced by The Bridgewater Book Company Ltd.

ISBN: 1-40543-159-8

Printed in China

NOTE

*This book uses metric and imperial measurements. Follow the same units of
measurement throughout; do not mix metric and imperial. All spoon measurements
are level: teaspoons are assumed to be 5 ml and tablespoons are assumed to be 15 ml.
Unless otherwise stated, milk is assumed to be full fat, eggs and individual vegetables
such as potatoes are medium, and pepper is freshly ground black pepper.*

*Ovens should be preheated to the specified temperature. If using a fan-assisted oven,
check the manufacturer's instructions for adjusting the time and temperature.*

*Recipes using raw or very lightly cooked eggs should be avoided by infants, the elderly,
pregnant women, convalescents and anyone suffering from an illness. Pregnant and
breastfeeding women are advised to avoid eating peanuts and peanut products.*

Contents

Introduction

Preparing food at home can give you a great sense of satisfaction, but it can seem something of a chore, and clearing up afterwards is often very tedious. Running a household, holding down a job and feeding the family can be difficult to balance, and with that hectic lifestyle, it is all too tempting to resort to unhealthy and expensive takeaways and convenience foods.

dishes, and they are also ideal complete meals for freezing. Finally, you can save even more time by keeping your storecupboard stocked up. The one-pot recipes in this book include everything from traditional stews, soups and bakes to more unusual dishes from the Middle East, Mexico and the Mediterranean and delicious desserts – dishes for every occasion.

One-pot meals meals are the ideal time-saving solution: they are more economical and healthier alternatives to convenience foods and are almost as easy, so why not try them for parties, Sunday lunches or family suppers? They make weekdays easier, create less washing-up and involve less preparation than many other

Less Mess

One-pot dishes are the ideal way of cutting down on the washing-up. They eliminate the need for extra saucepans or frying pans and several serving dishes – most of these recipes can be served straight from the cooking pot. Try to find an attractive set of casseroles that you can serve from at the table, whether cooking for the family or entertaining guests. Look for ones that are freezer- as well as oven-proof to save even more time and washing-up.

Freezing for the Future

Many one-pot meals can be frozen for future use: double the ingredients, and, when cooked, leave half to cool. Freeze in a rigid container, freezer-proof casserole or freezer bag for up to three months. To thaw, remove from the freezer 12 hours before you want your meal, leave at room temperature then heat in the microwave.

experiment by using ingredients buried at the back of the cupboard. Most of us keep the basics, such as pasta, rice and canned tomatoes, but next time you go shopping, spend some time in the canned food aisle and select a few more unusual ingredients to try in the future.

Stocking the Storecupboard

Although you can't beat the unique flavour and texture of fresh vegetables, there are alternatives that can make a delicious last-minute lunch or supper. Keep your cupboard well stocked to prevent a last-minute rush to the supermarket. Ingredients in jars or cans save on preparation time, too – most items can be bought chopped, peeled or flavoured at little or no extra cost. Improvise by using chickpeas when the recipe calls for kidney beans, and for new dishes

Equipment

Investing in good-quality equipment is important. Poor-quality pans and dishes do not cook food evenly, and are difficult to clean. The most important pans for one-pot cooking are lidded casserole dishes, saucepans and frying pans. When making casseroles and pot roasts, you need to select a dish large enough to give the ingredients room to cook, but not so much room that they dry out.

If you are planning to cook lots of casseroles and stews, a flameproof casserole is a good option. A solid, heavy-based casserole can be expensive, but is worth the cost, as the food will be evenly cooked and flavoursome. These pots can be used on the hob and in the oven. Cast-iron casseroles are best of all, but remember that they are very heavy when full.

Woks, frying pans and karahis (the Indian version of a wok) are also used for one-pot dishes, especially for stir-frying. Roasting tins are ideal for cooking one-pot roasts, with the vegetables sizzling in the juices from the meat. You may prefer a non-stick lining, but whatever type you choose, make sure that it is solid and large, and that the sides are of an adequate height, or you may find that the cooking juices drip dangerously over the rim.

You should think about the dishes you plan to cook and, therefore, the type of pan you will find most useful. If you cook on an electric hob with a flat surface, select a wok with a flat base, for example. A thick, solid base is important to allow even distribution of heat. If the manufacturer's instructions advise you to season a pan before you use it, do so, because this both improves the quality of cooking and extends the lifespan of the pan.

You will probably already have most of the other necessary utensils, but there may be some,

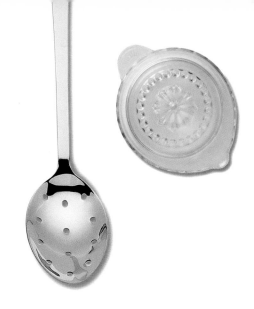

such as a zester, that you need to buy. Zesters are inexpensive and readily available. Using a zester is far easier than trying to grate lemon or orange rind then scrape it from the inside of the grater – and easier to clean, too. Chopping boards are an essential item and will last a long time. Whether you prefer wood or plastic, select a good, solid board that will not slip easily. Remember to use a separate board for raw meat. It is now thought that you should avoid cleaning utensils with anti-bacterial products, because various strains of bacteria can become completely resistant. Hot, soapy water is perfectly adequate for all pans and utensils; soak them first if there is any food stuck on the base.

Measuring jugs and spoons with clear, easy-to-read numbers are essential. Although you can estimate amounts with many casseroles and stews, some dishes require exact measurements. Make sure you have a full set of imperial or metric measuring equipment and, when following the recipes, remember to stick to one or the other: the two systems are not interchangeable.

Other tools you will need include a slotted spoon for draining and serving – very valuable in one-pot cooking when, for instance, you may need to remove the meat ahead of the sauce. Try to find a good set of plastic utensils for non-stick surfaces or stainless steel for other dishes – these will last for years. A pestle and mortar is another necessity if you want to use freshly ground spices; these will always add a better flavour and colour than ready-ground ones.

Good-quality, sharp knives make the cook's life a lot easier, saving time and increasing safety in the kitchen. You should also buy a knife sharpener and sharpen your knives regularly – using blunt knives is dangerous. A carving knife is ideal for carving pot roasts and other joints of meat. One large chopping knife with a heavy blade is useful for a multitude of purposes, but you may find a range of different sized knives suits you. A paring knife, being smaller and lighter, is perfect for trimming, peeling and chopping small vegetables.

Nowadays, there are ways to speed up preparation. For a real time-saver, invest in a food processor – a good-quality one will last for a long time. Alternatively, most supermarkets now stock washed, peeled and chopped raw vegetables, as well as their range of frozen and canned goods, which are a boon when you are short of time for preparing a meal. Canned foods never taste as good as raw ingredients and often have little texture and colour, but some, such as plum tomatoes and pulses, are invaluable.

Meat
& Fish

Cock-a-Leekie

Two for the price of one – serve the soup separately as a first course and the meat and vegetables as a main course. Alternatively, for a really chunky dish, ladle the whole thing into large soup plates.

serves 6

1.3 kg/3 lb chicken	salt and pepper
2.25 litres/4 pints beef stock	450 g/1 lb prunes, stoned and
900 g/2 lb leeks	soaked overnight in enough
1 bouquet garni	cold water to cover

Method

❶ Put the chicken, breast-side down, in a large, heavy-based saucepan or flameproof casserole. Pour in the stock and bring to the boil, skimming off any froth that rises to the surface.

❷ Tie half the leeks together in a bundle with kitchen string and thinly slice the remainder. Add the bundle of leeks to the saucepan with the bouquet garni and a pinch of salt. Reduce the heat, then partially cover and simmer for 2 hours, or until the chicken is tender.

❸ Remove and discard the bundle of leeks and bouquet garni. Drain the prunes, add them to the saucepan and simmer for 20 minutes. Season to taste, then add the sliced leeks. Simmer for a further 10 minutes. Slice the chicken, or cut into bite-sized pieces, and serve immediately.

Cook's tip

A bouquet garni usually consists of 3 fresh parsley sprigs, 2 fresh thyme sprigs and a bay leaf, tied together in a bundle.

Bacon & Lentil Soup

Bacon and lentils have a real affinity – their flavours and textures complement one another. This popular family supper also includes a selection of tasty winter vegetables.

serves 4–6

450 g/1 lb thick, rindless smoked
bacon rashers, diced

1 onion, chopped

2 carrots, sliced

2 celery sticks, chopped

1 turnip, chopped

1 large potato, chopped

85 g/3 oz Puy lentils

1 bouquet garni

1 litre/1¾ pints water or chicken stock

salt and pepper

Method

❶ Heat a large, heavy-based saucepan or flameproof casserole. Add the bacon and cook over a medium heat, stirring, for 4–5 minutes, or until the fat runs. Add the chopped onion, carrots, celery, turnip and potato and cook, stirring frequently, for 5 minutes.

❷ Add the lentils and bouquet garni and pour in the water. Bring to the boil, reduce the heat and simmer for 1 hour, or until the lentils are tender.

❸ Remove and discard the bouquet garni and season the soup to taste with pepper, and with salt, if necessary. Ladle into warmed soup bowls and serve immediately.

Cook's tip

Do not add any salt until the lentils have finished cooking, or they will toughen, which will impair the texture of the soup.

Beef & Vegetable Soup

This colourful, spicy soup comes from South-east Asia, where it would
be served with plain boiled rice, but it is substantial enough to make a
filling meal on its own.

serves 6

2 tbsp groundnut or sunflower oil

1 large onion, finely chopped

115 g/4 oz fresh lean beef mince

1 garlic clove, finely chopped

2 fresh red chillies, deseeded
and finely chopped

1 tbsp ground almonds

1 carrot, grated

1 tsp muscovado sugar

1-cm/½-inch cube shrimp paste (optional)

1 litre/1¾ pints chicken or beef stock

salt

115 g/4 oz cooked peeled prawns

225 g/8 oz fresh spinach, coarse stems
removed and leaves shredded

175 g/6 oz baby corn cobs, sliced

1 beef tomato, chopped

2 tbsp lime juice

Method

❶ Heat the oil in a large, heavy-based
saucepan. Add the onion and cook over
a low heat, stirring occasionally, for
5 minutes, or until softened. Add the beef
and garlic and cook, stirring, until the
meat is browned.

❷ Add the chillies, ground almonds,
grated carrot and sugar. Add the shrimp
paste (if using). Pour in the stock and
season to taste with salt. Bring the
mixture to the boil over a low heat,
then simmer for 10 minutes.

❸ Stir in the prawns, spinach, corn cobs,
tomato and lime juice. Simmer the
mixture for a further 2–3 minutes, or until
heated through. Ladle into warmed bowls
and serve immediately.

Variation

*Replace the prawns with 55 g/2 oz of dried shrimp
soaked in hot water for 10 minutes. Add the shrimp
and soaking water with the stock in Step 2.*

Beef Stroganoff

This traditional Slavic recipe makes a comforting meal on a chilly evening.
Thin strips of delicately cooked beef and a mustard and cream sauce make
this straightforward dish taste out of the ordinary.

serves 4

15 g/½ oz dried ceps

350 g/12 oz beef fillet

2 tbsp olive oil

115 g/4 oz shallots, sliced

175 g/6 oz chestnut mushrooms

salt and pepper

½ tsp Dijon mustard

5 tbsp double cream

fresh chives, to garnish

freshly cooked pasta, to serve

Method

❶ Put the dried ceps in a bowl and cover with hot water. Leave to soak for 20 minutes. Meanwhile, cut the beef against the grain into 5-mm/¼-inch thick slices, then into 1-cm/½-inch long strips, and reserve.

❷ Drain the ceps, reserving the soaking liquid, and chop. Sieve the soaking liquid through a fine-mesh sieve or coffee filter and reserve.

❸ Heat half the oil in a large frying pan. Add the shallots and cook over a low heat, stirring occasionally, for 5 minutes, or until softened. Add the soaked ceps, reserved soaking water and whole chestnut mushrooms. Cook, stirring frequently, for 10 minutes, or until almost all of the liquid has evaporated, then transfer the mixture to a plate.

❹ Heat the remaining oil in the frying pan, add the beef and cook, stirring frequently, for 4 minutes, or until browned all over. You may need to do this in batches. Return the mushroom mixture to the frying pan and season to taste. Put the mustard and cream in a small bowl and stir to mix, then fold into the mixture. Heat through gently, then serve with freshly cooked pasta, garnished with chives.

Beef in Beer with Herb Dumplings

Serve this traditional stew with its topping of satisfying dumplings to counteract even the coldest winter weather.

serves 6

2 tbsp sunflower oil

2 large onions, thinly sliced

8 carrots, sliced

4 tbsp plain flour

salt and pepper

1.25 kg/2 lb 12 oz stewing steak, cut into cubes

425 ml/15 fl oz stout

2 tsp muscovado sugar

2 bay leaves

1 tbsp chopped fresh thyme

Herb dumplings

115 g/4 oz self-raising flour

pinch of salt

55 g/2 oz shredded suet

2 tbsp chopped fresh parsley, plus extra to garnish

about 4 tbsp water

Method

❶ Preheat the oven to 160°C/325°F/ Gas Mark 3. Heat the oil in a flameproof casserole. Add the onions and carrots and cook over a low heat, stirring occasionally, for 5 minutes, or until the onions are softened. Meanwhile, put the flour in a polythene bag and season. Add the steak to the bag, tie the top and shake well to coat. Do this in batches, if necessary.

❷ Remove the vegetables from the casserole with a slotted spoon and reserve. Add the steak to the casserole, in batches, and cook, stirring frequently, until browned all over. Return the meat and the onions and carrots to the casserole and sprinkle in any remaining seasoned flour. Pour in the stout and add the sugar, bay leaves and thyme. Bring to the boil, cover and bake in the preheated oven for 1¾ hours.

❸ To make the Herb Dumplings, sift the flour and salt into a bowl. Stir in the suet and parsley, then add enough water to make a soft dough. Shape into small balls. Add to the casserole and return to the oven for 30 minutes. Remove and discard the bay leaves. Serve, sprinkled with parsley.

Stifado

This wonderful traditional Greek stew is cooked very slowly with the result
that the beef almost melts in the mouth and all the flavours mingle in a rich,
thick, delicious gravy.

serves 6

450 g/1 lb tomatoes, peeled

150 ml/5 fl oz beef stock

2 tbsp olive oil

450 g/1 lb shallots, peeled

2 garlic cloves, finely chopped

700 g/1 lb 9 oz stewing steak,
cut into 2.5-cm/1-inch cubes

1 fresh rosemary sprig

1 bay leaf

2 tbsp red wine vinegar

salt and pepper

450 g/1 lb potatoes, quartered

Method

❶ Put the tomatoes in a blender or food
processor, add the stock and process to a
purée. Alternatively, push them through
a sieve into a bowl with the back of a
wooden spoon and mix with the stock.

❷ Heat the oil in a large, heavy-based
saucepan or flameproof casserole. Add
the shallots and garlic and cook over a low
heat, stirring occasionally, for 8 minutes,
or until golden. Transfer to a plate with
a slotted spoon. Add the steak to the
saucepan and cook, stirring frequently,
for 5–8 minutes, or until browned.

❸ Return the shallots and garlic to the
saucepan, add the tomato mixture, herbs
and vinegar and season to taste. Cover
and simmer gently for 1½ hours. Add the
potatoes, re-cover and simmer for a
further 30 minutes. Remove and discard
the rosemary and bay leaf and serve.

Cook's tip

*Fresh, uncooked rosemary sprigs and bay leaves
would make an attractive garnish for this dish, but
remember to remove them before eating.*

Irish Stew

Nothing could be simpler, tastier or more economical than this traditional, heart-warming stew. Serve with fresh soda bread for an authentic touch – and to mop up the delicious juices.

serves 4

4 tbsp plain flour

salt and pepper

1.3 kg/3 lb middle neck of lamb,
cut into cutlet-sized pieces and
trimmed of excess fat

3 large onions, chopped

3 carrots, sliced

450 g/1 lb potatoes, quartered

½ tsp dried thyme

850 ml/1½ pints beef stock

2 tbsp chopped fresh parsley,
to garnish

Method

❶ Preheat the oven to 160°C/325°F/ Gas Mark 3. Spread the flour on a plate and season. Roll the pieces of lamb in the flour to coat, shaking off any excess, and arrange in the base of a casserole.

❷ Layer the onions, carrots and potatoes on top of the lamb.

❸ Sprinkle in the thyme and pour in the stock, then cover and cook in the preheated oven for 2½ hours. Garnish with the chopped fresh parsley and serve straight from the casserole.

Cook's tip

This stew is even more substantial and flavoursome if it is served with Herb Dumplings (see page 18). Add them to the casserole 30 minutes before the end of the cooking time.

Moroccan Lamb

Slow-cooking lamb with dried fruit and spices is traditional in North Africa. Stews flavoured with dried fruits, including apricots and prunes, have now become familiar elsewhere.

serves 4

500 g/1 lb 2 oz boneless leg of lamb	½ tsp saffron threads, lightly crushed
1 tbsp sunflower oil	¼ tsp freshly grated nutmeg
350 g/12 oz shallots, peeled but left whole	salt and pepper
425 ml/15 fl oz chicken stock	grated rind and juice of 1 small orange,
1 tbsp clear honey	plus extra rind to garnish
1 tsp ground cinnamon	12 no-soak dried prunes
½ tsp ground ginger	

Method

❶ Cut the lamb into large cubes. Heat the oil in a flameproof casserole, then add the lamb and cook over a medium heat, stirring, for 3–5 minutes, or until browned. Transfer to a plate. Add the shallots to the casserole and cook over a low heat, stirring occasionally, for 10 minutes, or until golden. Transfer them to a separate plate with a slotted spoon.

❷ Pour away any excess fat from the casserole, then add the stock and bring to the boil, stirring constantly and scraping up any sediment from the base. Return the lamb to the casserole and stir in the honey, cinnamon, ginger, saffron and nutmeg. Season to taste, then cover and simmer for 30 minutes.

❸ Return the shallots to the casserole and add the orange rind and juice. Re-cover and simmer for a further 30 minutes. Add the prunes and adjust the seasoning, if necessary. Simmer, uncovered, for a further 15 minutes. Garnish with orange rind and serve immediately.

Cook's tip

'No-soak' dried fruit requires no advance preparation. You can also find bags of moist, 'ready-to-eat' fruit in most supermarkets.

French Country Casserole

A crispy potato topping covers a dish of succulent, tender lamb, flavoured
with mint, leeks and apricots in this traditional rustic casserole – which tastes
as good as it looks.

serves 6

2 tbsp sunflower oil

2 kg/4 lb 8 oz boneless leg of lamb,
cut into 2.5-cm/1-inch cubes

6 leeks, sliced

1 tbsp plain flour

150 ml/5 fl oz rosé wine

300 ml/10 fl oz chicken stock

1 tbsp tomato purée

1 tbsp sugar

2 tbsp chopped fresh mint

115 g/4 oz dried apricots, chopped

salt and pepper

1 kg/2 lb 4 oz potatoes, sliced

3 tbsp melted unsalted butter

fresh mint sprigs, to garnish

Method

❶ Preheat the oven to 180°C/350°F/
Gas Mark 4. Heat the oil in a large,
flameproof casserole. Add the lamb in
batches and cook over a medium heat,
stirring, for 5–8 minutes, or until browned.
Transfer to a plate.

❷ Add the sliced leeks to the casserole
and cook, stirring occasionally, for
5 minutes, or until softened. Sprinkle in
the flour and cook, stirring, for 1 minute.
Pour in the wine and stock and bring to
the boil, stirring. Stir in the tomato purée,
sugar, chopped mint and apricots and
season to taste.

❸ Return the lamb to the casserole and
stir. Arrange the potato slices on top and
brush with the melted butter. Cover and
bake in the preheated oven for 1½ hours.

❹ Increase the oven temperature to
200°C/400°F/Gas Mark 6, then uncover
the casserole and bake for a further
30 minutes, or until the potato topping
is golden brown. Serve immediately,
garnished with fresh mint sprigs.

Paprika Pork

This is a good dish for entertaining, as it can be prepared in advance and stored in the refrigerator for up to two days. To serve, reheat gently, then stir in the soured cream.

serves 4

675 g/1 lb 8 oz pork fillet

2 tbsp sunflower oil

25 g/1 oz butter

1 onion, chopped

1 tbsp paprika

25 g/1 oz plain flour

300 ml/10 fl oz chicken stock

4 tbsp dry sherry

115 g/4 oz mushrooms, sliced

salt and pepper

150 ml/5 fl oz soured cream

Method

❶ Cut the pork into 4-cm/1½-inch cubes. Heat the oil and butter in a large saucepan. Add the pork and cook over a medium heat, stirring, for 5 minutes, or until browned. Transfer to a plate with a slotted spoon.

❷ Add the chopped onion to the saucepan and cook, stirring occasionally, for 5 minutes, or until softened. Stir in the paprika and flour and cook, stirring constantly, for 2 minutes. Gradually stir in the stock and bring to the boil, stirring constantly.

❸ Return the pork to the saucepan, add the sherry and sliced mushrooms and season to taste. Cover and simmer gently for 20 minutes, or until the pork is tender. Stir in the soured cream and serve.

Cook's tip

There are 2 kinds of paprika – sweet and hot – but both are much milder than cayenne pepper. Sweet paprika is the best choice for this recipe.

Pot-roast Pork

Beef and chicken are the most popular choices for pot roasting, but a loin of pork works superbly well, too. This is a rich and flavoursome dish that is ideal for entertaining.

serves 4

1 tbsp sunflower oil

55 g/2 oz butter

1 kg/2 lb 4 oz boned and rolled pork loin

4 shallots, chopped

6 juniper berries

2 fresh thyme sprigs, plus extra to garnish

150 ml/5 fl oz dry cider

150 ml/5 fl oz chicken stock or water

salt and pepper

8 celery sticks, chopped

2 tbsp plain flour

150 ml/5 fl oz double cream

freshly cooked peas, to serve

Method

❶ Heat the oil with half the butter in a heavy-based saucepan or flameproof casserole. Add the pork and cook over a medium heat, turning frequently, for 5–10 minutes, or until browned. Transfer to a plate.

❷ Add the shallots to the saucepan and cook, stirring frequently, for 5 minutes, or until softened. Add the juniper berries and thyme sprigs and return the pork to the saucepan, with any juices that have collected on the plate. Pour in the cider and stock, season to taste, then cover and simmer for 30 minutes. Turn the pork over and then add the celery. Re-cover the pan and then cook for a further 40 minutes.

❸ Meanwhile, make a beurre manié by mashing the remaining butter with the flour in a small bowl. Transfer the pork and celery to a platter with a slotted spoon and keep warm. Remove and discard the juniper berries and thyme.

❹ Whisk the beurre manié, a little at a time, into the simmering cooking liquid. Cook, stirring constantly, for 2 minutes, then stir in the cream and bring to the boil. Slice the pork and spoon a little of the sauce over it. Garnish with thyme sprigs and serve immediately with the celery and freshly cooked peas. Hand round the remaining sauce separately.

Brunswick Stew

This traditional chicken stew is a hearty dish, which is suffused with warm, spicy undertones. Serve it with salad and wholemeal rolls to make a filling, warming winter supper.

serves 6

1.8 kg/4 lb chicken pieces

salt

2 tbsp paprika

2 tbsp olive oil

25 g/1 oz butter

450 g/1 lb onions, chopped

2 yellow peppers, deseeded and chopped

400 g/14 oz canned chopped tomatoes

225 ml/8 fl oz dry white wine

450 ml/16 fl oz chicken stock

1 tbsp Worcestershire sauce

½ tsp Tabasco sauce

1 tbsp finely chopped fresh parsley

325 g/11½ oz canned sweetcorn kernels, drained

425 g/15 oz canned butter beans, drained and rinsed

2 tbsp plain flour

4 tbsp water

fresh parsley sprigs, to garnish

Method

❶ Season the chicken pieces with salt and dust with paprika.

❷ Heat the oil and butter in a flameproof casserole or large saucepan. Add the chicken pieces and cook over a medium heat, turning, for 10–15 minutes, or until golden. Transfer the chicken to a plate using a slotted spoon.

❸ Add the onion and peppers to the casserole. Cook over a low heat, stirring occasionally, for 5 minutes, or until softened. Add the tomatoes, wine, stock, Worcestershire sauce, Tabasco sauce and parsley and bring to the boil, stirring. Return the chicken to the casserole, then cover and simmer, stirring occasionally, for 30 minutes.

❹ Add the sweetcorn and beans to the casserole, partially re-cover and simmer for a further 30 minutes. Put the flour and water in a small bowl and mix to make a paste. Stir a ladleful of the cooking liquid into the paste, then stir it into the stew. Cook, stirring frequently, for 5 minutes. Serve, garnished with parsley.

Jambalaya

This Cajun dish is borrowed from Spain, where it originated. Its lively mixture of chicken and prawns makes it a good dish to serve at a brunch party, instead of the more traditional kedgeree.

serves 6

2 tbsp lard

1.5 kg/3 lb 5 oz chicken pieces

25 g/1 oz plain flour

225 g/8 oz rindless smoked gammon, diced

1 onion, chopped

1 orange pepper, deseeded and sliced

350 g/12 oz tomatoes, peeled and chopped

1 garlic clove, finely chopped

1 tsp chopped fresh thyme

12 Mediterranean prawns, peeled

225 g/8 oz long-grain rice

450 ml/16 fl oz chicken stock or water

dash of Tabasco sauce

salt and pepper

3 spring onions, finely chopped

2 tbsp chopped fresh flat-leaved parsley

fresh flat-leaved parsley sprigs, to garnish

Method

❶ Melt the lard in a large, flameproof casserole. Add the chicken and cook over a medium heat, turning occasionally, for 8–10 minutes, or until golden brown all over. Transfer the chicken to a plate using a slotted spoon.

❷ Add the flour and cook over a very low heat, stirring, for 15 minutes, or until golden brown. Do not let it burn. Return the chicken pieces to the casserole with the gammon, onion, orange pepper, tomatoes, garlic and thyme. Cook, stirring frequently, for 10 minutes.

❸ Stir in the prawns, rice and stock and season to taste with Tabasco, salt and pepper. Bring the mixture to the boil, then reduce the heat and cook for 15–20 minutes, or until all of the liquid has been absorbed and the rice is tender. Stir in the spring onions and chopped parsley, garnish with parsley sprigs and serve immediately.

Variation

If you don't want to use lard in this recipe, substitute 2 tablespoons of corn oil at the beginning of Step 1.

Chicken Pasanda

This Balti dish is traditionally cooked and served in a karahi – a pan similar in shape to a wok. If you have neither a karahi nor a wok, use a large, heavy-based frying pan instead.

serves 4

4 cardamom pods	675 g/1 lb 8 oz skinless, boneless
6 black peppercorns	chicken, diced
½ cinnamon stick	5 tbsp groundnut oil
½ tsp cumin seeds	2 onions, finely chopped
2 tsp garam masala	3 fresh green chillies, deseeded
1 tsp chilli powder	and chopped
1 tsp grated fresh root ginger	2 tbsp chopped fresh coriander
1 garlic clove, very finely chopped	125 ml/4 fl oz single cream
4 tbsp thick natural yogurt	fresh coriander sprigs, to garnish
pinch of salt	

Method

❶ Put the cardamom pods in a non-metallic dish with the peppercorns, cinnamon, cumin, garam masala, chilli powder, ginger, garlic, yogurt and salt. Add the chicken pieces and stir well to coat. Cover and leave to marinate in the refrigerator for 2–3 hours.

❷ Heat the oil in a preheated wok or karahi. Add the onions and cook over a low heat, stirring occasionally, for 5 minutes, or until softened, then add the chicken pieces and marinade and cook over a medium heat, stirring, for 15 minutes, or until the chicken is cooked through.

❸ Stir in the fresh chillies and coriander and pour in the cream. Heat through gently, but do not let it boil. Garnish with fresh coriander and serve immediately.

Coq au Vin

Traditional recipes often yield wonderfully tasty results, and this dish is no exception. Serve this perennial favourite with warm French bread or garlic bread to mop up the delicious wine-flavoured juices.

serves 4

55 g/2 oz butter

2 tbsp olive oil

1.8 kg/4 lb chicken pieces

115 g/4 oz rindless smoked bacon, cut into strips

115 g/4 oz baby onions

115 g/4 oz chestnut mushrooms, halved

2 garlic cloves, finely chopped

2 tbsp brandy

225 ml/8 fl oz red wine

300 ml/10 fl oz chicken stock

1 bouquet garni

salt and pepper

2 tbsp plain flour

bay leaves, to garnish

Method

❶ Melt half the butter with the olive oil in a large, flameproof casserole. Add the chicken and cook over a medium heat, stirring, for 8–10 minutes, or until golden brown all over. Add the bacon, onions, mushrooms and garlic.

❷ Pour in the brandy and set it alight with a match or taper. When the flames have died down, add the wine, stock and bouquet garni and season to taste. Bring to the boil, reduce the heat and simmer gently for 1 hour, or until the chicken pieces are cooked through and tender. Meanwhile, make a beurre manié by mashing the remaining butter with the flour in a small bowl.

❸ Remove and discard the bouquet garni. Transfer the chicken to a large plate and keep warm. Stir the beurre manié into the casserole, a little at a time. Bring to the boil, return the chicken to the casserole and serve immediately, garnished with bay leaves.

Cook's tip

If you like, cook the chicken in the oven instead of on the hob. Transfer it to a preheated oven, 160°C/325°F/Gas Mark 3, once the mixture has come to the boil in Step 2. Cook for 1 hour, then follow Step 3.

Mexican Turkey

Using chocolate in savoury dishes is a Mexican tradition and, while it may sound strange, it gives the meat a very rich flavour. Mexican chocolate often has cinnamon incorporated into it, but you can use ordinary plain chocolate and ground cinnamon for this dish.

serves 4

55 g/2 oz plain flour

salt and pepper

4 turkey breast fillets

3 tbsp corn oil

1 onion, thinly sliced

1 red pepper, deseeded and sliced

300 ml/10 fl oz chicken stock

25 g/1 oz raisins

4 tomatoes, peeled, deseeded and chopped

1 tsp chilli powder

½ tsp ground cinnamon

pinch of ground cumin

25 g/1 oz plain chocolate, finely chopped or grated

chopped fresh coriander, to garnish

Method

❶ Preheat the oven to 160°C/325°F/ Gas Mark 3. Spread the flour on a plate and season. Coat the turkey fillets in the seasoned flour, shaking off any excess.

❷ Heat the oil in a flameproof casserole. Add the turkey fillets and cook over a medium heat, turning occasionally, for 5–10 minutes, or until golden. Transfer to a plate using a slotted spoon.

❸ Add the onion and red pepper to the casserole. Cook over a low heat, stirring occasionally, for 5 minutes, or until softened. Sprinkle in any remaining seasoned flour and cook, stirring constantly, for 1 minute. Gradually stir in the stock, then add the raisins, chopped tomatoes, chilli powder, cinnamon, cumin and chocolate. Season to taste. Bring to the boil, stirring constantly.

❹ Return the turkey to the casserole, cover and cook in the preheated oven for 50 minutes. Serve immediately, garnished with coriander.

Cook's tip

For true flavour, choose the best-quality plain chocolate you can find for this dish. It should contain a minimum of 70 per cent cocoa solids.

Italian Turkey Steaks

This lively summer dish is simplicity itself, but tastes really wonderful and makes a surprisingly substantial main course.

serves 4

1 tbsp olive oil

4 turkey escalopes or steaks

2 red peppers

1 red onion

2 garlic cloves, finely chopped

300 ml/10 fl oz passata

150 ml/5 fl oz medium white wine

1 tbsp chopped fresh marjoram

salt and pepper

400 g/14 oz canned cannellini beans, drained and rinsed

3 tbsp fresh white breadcrumbs

fresh basil sprigs, to garnish

Method

❶ Heat the oil in a flameproof casserole or heavy-based frying pan. Add the turkey escalopes and cook over a medium heat for 5–10 minutes, turning occasionally, until golden. Transfer to a plate.

❷ Deseed and slice the red peppers. Slice the onion, add to the frying pan with the red peppers and cook over a low heat, stirring occasionally, for 5 minutes, or until softened. Add the garlic and cook for a further 2 minutes.

❸ Return the turkey to the frying pan and add the passata, wine and marjoram. Season to taste with salt and pepper. Bring to the boil, then reduce the heat, cover and simmer, stirring occasionally, for 25–30 minutes, or until the turkey is cooked through and tender.

❹ Preheat the grill. Stir in the cannellini beans and simmer for a further 5 minutes. Sprinkle the breadcrumbs over the top and cook under the hot grill for 2–3 minutes, or until golden. Serve, garnished with fresh basil sprigs.

Variation

Soak 15 g/½ oz of dried porcini mushrooms in boiling water to cover for 20 minutes. Drain and slice, then add with the onion and peppers in Step 2.

Seafood Risotto

The secret of a successful risotto is to use round grain Italian rice, such as arborio, and to add a ladleful of stock at a time, making sure that it is fully absorbed before more is added.

serves 4

350 g/12 oz skinless cod fillet

25 g/1 oz unsalted butter

1 onion, chopped

2 red peppers, deseeded and chopped

4 tomatoes, peeled, deseeded and chopped

8 ready-prepared scallops

2 tbsp olive oil

225 g/8 oz risotto rice

450 ml/16 fl oz hot fish stock

salt

225 g/8 oz cooked peeled prawns

1 tbsp chopped flat-leaved parsley

2 tbsp freshly grated Parmesan cheese

fresh parsley sprigs, to garnish

Method

❶ Cut the fish into cubes. Melt half the butter in a large saucepan. Add the onion, red peppers and tomatoes and then cook over a low heat, stirring occasionally, for 5 minutes, or until softened. Add the fish and scallops, and cook for a further 3 minutes. Transfer the fish mixture to a plate using a slotted spoon, then cover and reserve.

❷ Add the oil and the remaining butter to the pan and heat gently. Add the rice and stir to coat with the butter and oil. Stir in a ladleful of stock and season to taste with salt. Cook, stirring, until the stock has been absorbed. Continue cooking and adding stock, a ladleful at a time, for 20 minutes, or until the rice is tender and all of the liquid has been absorbed.

❸ Gently stir in the reserved fish mixture with the prawns and heat through for 2 minutes. Transfer the risotto to a warmed serving dish, sprinkle with the parsley and Parmesan cheese and serve immediately, garnished with parsley sprigs.

Cook's tip

Risotto rice will absorb stock more readily if the stock is kept at simmering point in another saucepan while it is being added in Step 2.

Thai Prawn Curry

Thai cooking is renowned for its subtle blending of aromatic
spices, and this mouthwatering curry is no exception.

serves 4

450 g/1 lb raw tiger prawns

2 tbsp groundnut oil

2 tbsp Thai green curry paste

4 kaffir lime leaves, shredded

1 lemon grass stalk, chopped

225 ml/8 fl oz coconut milk

2 tbsp Thai fish sauce

½ cucumber, deseeded and cut into batons

12 fresh basil leaves, plus extra to garnish

2 fresh green chillies, sliced

Method

❶ Peel and devein the prawns. Heat the
groundnut oil in a preheated wok or
heavy-based frying pan. Add the curry
paste and cook over a medium heat for
1 minute, or until it is bubbling and
releases its aroma.

❷ Add the prawns, lime leaves and lemon
grass and stir-fry for 2 minutes,
or until the prawns have turned pink.

❸ Stir in the coconut milk and bring to
the boil, then reduce the heat and simmer,
stirring occasionally, for 5 minutes. Stir in
the fish sauce, cucumber and basil.
Transfer to a warmed serving dish. Scatter
over the chilli slices, garnish with fresh
basil leaves and serve.

Cook's tip

Three types of basil are used in Thailand: hairy
(bai mangluk), *sweet* (bai horapa) *and Thai or holy
basil* (bai grapao). *They are all more strongly
flavoured than Western basil.*

Paella del Mar

Paella is actually the name of the pan in which this famous Spanish dish is cooked – a large, heavy-based frying pan or casserole is a good substitute.

serves 6

450 g/1 lb live mussels

6 squid

125 ml/4 fl oz olive oil

1 Spanish onion, chopped

2 garlic cloves, finely chopped

1 red pepper, deseeded and cut into strips

1 green pepper, deseeded and cut into strips

400 g/14 oz risotto rice

2 tomatoes, peeled and chopped

1 tbsp tomato purée

175 g/6 oz monkfish fillet, cut into chunks

175 g/6 oz red mullet fillet, cut into chunks

175 g/6 oz cod fillet, cut into chunks

500 ml/18 fl oz fish stock

115 g/4 oz fresh or frozen green beans, halved

115 g/4 oz fresh or frozen peas

6 canned artichoke hearts, drained

¼ tsp saffron threads

salt and pepper

12 raw Mediterranean or tiger prawns

Method

❶ Clean the mussels by scrubbing the shells and pulling off any beards. Discard any with broken shells or any that refuse to close when tapped with a knife. Rinse the mussels under cold running water.

❷ To prepare each squid, pull the pouch and tentacles apart, then remove the innards from the pouch. Slice the tentacles away from the head and discard the head. Rinse the pouch and tentacles under cold running water.

❸ Heat the oil in a paella pan. Add the onion, garlic and peppers and cook over a medium heat, stirring, for 5 minutes, or until softened. Add the squid and cook for 2 minutes. Add the rice and cook, stirring, until transparent and coated with oil.

❹ Add the tomatoes, tomato purée and fish and cook for 3 minutes, then add the stock. Stir in the beans, peas, artichoke hearts and saffron and season to taste.

❺ Arrange the mussels around the edge of the pan, then top the mixture with the prawns. Bring to the boil, reduce the heat and simmer, shaking the pan from time to time, for 15–20 minutes, or until the rice is tender. Discard any mussels that remain closed. Serve straight from the pan.

Moules Marinières

Served with plenty of fresh crusty French bread, this is a shellfish-lover's feast.
The only extra treat you need to make this into a perfect meal is a glass of
chilled white wine.

serves 4

2 kg/4 lb 8 oz live mussels

300 ml/10 fl oz dry white wine

6 shallots, finely chopped

1 bouquet garni

pepper

crusty bread, to serve

Method

❶ Clean the mussels by scrubbing the shells and pulling off any beards. Discard any with broken shells or any that refuse to close when tapped with a knife. Rinse the mussels under cold running water.

❷ Pour the wine into a large, heavy-based saucepan, add the shallots and bouquet garni and season to taste with pepper. Bring to the boil over a medium heat. Add the mussels, cover tightly and cook, shaking the saucepan occasionally, for 5 minutes. Remove and discard the bouquet garni and any mussels that remain closed.

❸ Divide the mussels between 4 soup plates with a slotted spoon. Tilt the casserole to let any sand settle, then spoon the cooking liquid over the mussels and serve immediately with bread.

Cook's tip

Never eat mussels that you have collected from the beach yourself, as they may have been polluted and could cause serious illness.

Boston Fish Pie

The Massachusetts city of Boston has been described as 'the home of the bean and the cod'. This may not sound glamorous, but this unusual fish pie does demonstrate that it is a tasty and filling combination.

serves 6

25 g/1 oz butter, plus extra for greasing

2 onions, chopped

1 kg/2 lb 4 oz cod fillet, skinned and cut into strips

4 rindless streaky bacon rashers, cut into strips

2 tbsp chopped fresh parsley

salt and pepper

400 g/14 oz canned haricot beans, drained and rinsed

600 ml/1 pint milk

500 g/1 lb 2 oz potatoes, very thinly sliced

fresh parsley sprigs, to garnish

Method

❶ Preheat the oven to 180°C/350°F/ Gas Mark 4. Lightly grease a flameproof casserole with a little butter. Arrange the chopped onions in the base and then cover with the strips of fish and bacon. Sprinkle with the chopped parsley and season to taste.

❷ Add the haricot beans, then pour in the milk. Arrange the potato slices, overlapping them slightly, to cover the entire surface of the pie.

❸ Dot the potato slices with the butter. Bake the pie in the preheated oven for 40 minutes, or until the potatoes are crisp and golden. Garnish with parsley sprigs and serve immediately.

Cook's tip

If you like, before baking in the oven, cover the casserole with aluminium foil, then remove the foil for the last 10 minutes of cooking time to crisp up the potatoes.

Vegetarian

Sweetcorn, Potato & Cheese Soup

This easy-to-make, satisfying soup is put together mainly with storecupboard ingredients. It is the perfect choice for a Sunday brunch, as it takes very little effort or concentration.

serves 4

25 g/1 oz butter

2 shallots, finely chopped

225 g/8 oz potatoes, diced

4 tbsp plain flour

2 tbsp dry white wine

300 ml/10 fl oz milk

325 g/11½ oz canned sweetcorn, drained

85 g/3 oz Gruyère, Emmenthal or Cheddar cheese, grated

8–10 fresh sage leaves, chopped

425 ml/15 fl oz double cream

fresh sage sprigs, to garnish

Croûtons

2–3 slices of day-old white bread

2 tbsp olive oil

Method

❶ To make the croûtons, cut the crusts off the slices of bread, then cut the remaining bread into 5-mm/¼-inch squares. Heat the olive oil in a heavy-based frying pan and add the bread cubes. Cook, tossing and stirring constantly, until evenly coloured. Drain the croûtons thoroughly on kitchen paper and reserve.

❷ Melt the butter in a large, heavy-based saucepan. Add the shallots and cook over a low heat, stirring occasionally, for 5 minutes, or until softened. Add the potatoes and cook, stirring, for 2 minutes.

❸ Sprinkle in the flour and cook, stirring, for 1 minute. Remove the saucepan from the heat and stir in the white wine, then gradually stir in the milk. Return the saucepan to the heat and bring to the boil, stirring constantly, then reduce the heat and simmer.

❹ Stir in the sweetcorn kernels, grated cheese, chopped sage and cream and heat through gently until the cheese has just melted. Ladle the soup into warmed bowls, scatter over the croûtons, garnish with fresh sage sprigs and serve immediately.

Cauliflower Bake

The bright red of the tomatoes is a great contrast to the colours of the cauliflower and herbs in this dish, making it appealing to both the eye and the palate. It is easy to prepare and satisfying to eat.

serves 4

500 g/1 lb 2 oz cauliflower,
broken into florets

600 g/1 lb 5 oz potatoes, cut into cubes

100 g/3½ oz cherry tomatoes

chopped fresh flat-leaved parsley,
to garnish

Sauce

25 g/1 oz butter or margarine

1 leek, sliced

1 garlic clove, crushed

3 tbsp plain flour

300 ml/10 fl oz milk

85 g/3 oz mixed cheese, such as Cheddar,
Parmesan and Gruyère, grated

½ tsp paprika

2 tbsp chopped fresh flat-leaved parsley

salt and pepper

Method

❶ Preheat the oven to 180°C/350°F/ Gas Mark 4. Cook the cauliflower florets in a saucepan of boiling water for 10 minutes. Meanwhile, cook the potato cubes in a saucepan of boiling water for 10 minutes. Drain both vegetables and reserve.

❷ To make the sauce, melt the butter in a large saucepan, add the leek and garlic and cook over a low heat for 1 minute. Stir in the flour and cook, stirring constantly, for 1 minute. Remove the saucepan from the heat, then gradually stir in the milk, 55 g/2 oz of the cheese,

the paprika and the parsley. Return the saucepan to the heat and bring to the boil, stirring constantly. Season to taste.

❸ Transfer the cauliflower to a deep, ovenproof dish with the cherry tomatoes, and top with the potatoes. Pour the sauce over the potatoes and sprinkle over the remaining grated cheese.

❹ Cook in the preheated oven for 20 minutes, or until the vegetables are cooked through and the cheese is golden brown and bubbling. Garnish with chopped parsley and serve immediately.

Pepper &
Mushroom Hash

This quick and easy-to-prepare one-pan dish is ideal for an evening snack. Packed
with colour and flavour, it is an extremely versatile recipe – you can add whichever
vegetables you have to hand.

serves 4

675 g/1 lb 8 oz potatoes, cut into cubes

1 tbsp olive oil

2 garlic cloves, crushed

1 green pepper, deseeded and cut
into cubes

1 yellow pepper, deseeded and cut
into cubes

3 tomatoes, diced

75 g/2¾ oz button mushrooms, halved

1 tbsp Worcestershire sauce

salt and pepper

2 tbsp chopped fresh basil

fresh basil sprigs, to garnish

warm crusty bread, to serve

Method

❶ Cook the potato cubes in a saucepan
of lightly salted boiling water for
7–8 minutes. Drain well and reserve.

❷ Heat the olive oil in a large, heavy-
based frying pan. Add the potato cubes
and cook over a medium heat, stirring, for
8–10 minutes, or until browned.

❸ Add the crushed garlic and pepper
cubes and cook, stirring frequently, for
2–3 minutes. Add the tomatoes and
mushrooms and cook, stirring frequently,
for 5–6 minutes.

❹ Stir in the Worcestershire sauce and
basil and season to taste with salt and
pepper. Transfer to a warmed serving dish,
garnish with basil leaves and serve with
warm crusty bread.

Cook's tip

*Most brands of Worcestershire sauce contain
anchovies, so if you are a vegetarian, check the
label to make sure you choose a vegetarian variety.*

Winter Cobbler

Seasonal vegetables are casseroled with lentils then topped with cheese scones.

serves 4

1 tbsp olive oil

1 garlic clove, crushed

8 small onions, halved

2 celery sticks, sliced

225 g/8 oz swede, chopped

½ small cauliflower, broken into florets

2 carrots, sliced

225 g/8 oz mushrooms, sliced

400 g/14 oz canned chopped tomatoes

55 g/2 oz red split lentils, rinsed

2 tbsp cornflour

3–4 tbsp water

300 ml/10 fl oz vegetable stock

2 tsp Tabasco sauce

2 tsp chopped fresh oregano

fresh oregano sprigs, to garnish

Topping

225 g/8 oz self-raising flour

pinch of salt

4 tbsp butter

115 g/4 oz mature Cheddar cheese, grated

2 tsp chopped fresh oregano

1 egg, lightly beaten

150 ml/5 fl oz milk

Method

❶ Preheat the oven to 180°C/350°F/ Gas Mark 4. Heat the olive oil in a large frying pan and cook the garlic and onions over a low heat for 5 minutes. Add the celery, swede, cauliflower florets and carrots to the frying pan and cook for 2–3 minutes.

❷ Add the mushrooms, tomatoes and lentils to the frying pan. Put the cornflour and water in a bowl and mix to make a smooth paste. Stir into the frying pan with the vegetable stock, Tabasco and oregano. Transfer to an ovenproof dish, cover and bake in the preheated oven for 20 minutes.

❸ To make the topping, sift the flour and salt into a bowl. Rub in the butter, then stir in most of the cheese and the chopped oregano. Beat the egg with the milk in a small bowl and add enough to the dry ingredients to make a soft dough. Knead, then roll out to 1-cm/½-inch thick and cut into 5-cm/2-inch rounds.

❹ Remove the dish from the oven and increase the temperature to 200°C/400°F/ Gas Mark 6. Arrange the dough around the edge, brush with the remaining egg mixture and sprinkle with the reserved cheese. Cook for 10–12 minutes. Garnish with oregano sprigs and serve.

Potato-topped Vegetables

This dish is packed full of crunchy vegetables and coated in a white wine sauce.

serves 4

1 carrot, diced

175 g/6 oz cauliflower florets

175 g/6 oz broccoli florets

1 fennel bulb, sliced

85 g/3 oz French beans, halved

25 g/1 oz butter

25 g/1 oz plain flour

150 ml/5 fl oz vegetable stock

150 ml/5 fl oz dry white wine

150 ml/5 fl oz milk

175 g/6 oz chestnut mushrooms, quartered

2 tbsp chopped fresh sage

Topping

900 g/2 lb floury potatoes, diced

25 g/1 oz butter

4 tbsp natural yogurt

70 g/2½ oz freshly grated Parmesan cheese

1 tsp fennel seeds

salt and pepper

Method

❶ Preheat the oven to 190°C/375°F/ Gas Mark 5. Cook the carrot, cauliflower, broccoli, fennel and beans in a saucepan of boiling water for 10 minutes, or until just tender. Drain the vegetables and reserve.

❷ Melt the butter in a saucepan. Stir in the flour and cook over a low heat for 1 minute. Remove from the heat and stir in the stock, wine and milk. Return to the heat and bring to the boil, stirring, until thickened. Stir in the reserved vegetables, mushrooms and chopped sage.

❸ To make the topping, cook the diced potatoes in a saucepan of boiling salted water for 10–15 minutes. Drain and mash with the butter, yogurt and half the Parmesan cheese. Stir in the fennel seeds and season to taste.

❹ Spoon the vegetable mixture into a 1-litre/1¾-pint pie dish. Spoon the potato mixture over the top, sprinkle over the remaining cheese and cook in the preheated oven for 30–35 minutes, or until golden. Serve immediately.

Risotto Primavera

As evenings get longer, the days grow warmer and the first spring vegetables ripen, this is the ideal choice for a midweek supper.

serves 4

115 g/4 oz asparagus spears, cut into short lengths

2 young carrots, thinly sliced

25 g/1 oz unsalted butter

2 tbsp olive oil

1 white onion, chopped

2 garlic cloves, finely chopped

225 g/8 oz risotto rice

3 tbsp dry white wine

1 litre/1¾ pints hot vegetable stock

55 g/2 oz button mushrooms, halved

salt and pepper

55 g/2 oz freshly grated Parmesan cheese, to serve

Method

❶ Blanch the asparagus and carrots in a large saucepan of boiling water and drain well.

❷ Melt the butter with the oil in a large, heavy-based saucepan. Add the onion and garlic and cook over a low heat, stirring occasionally, for 5 minutes, or until softened. Add the rice and stir well to coat the grains with the butter and oil. Add the white wine and cook until the liquid has been fully absorbed.

❸ Add a ladleful of stock to the rice and cook, stirring, until the liquid has been absorbed. Continue cooking and adding the stock, a ladleful at a time, for 20 minutes, or until the rice is tender and all of the liquid has been absorbed.

❹ Gently stir in the asparagus, carrots and mushrooms, season to taste and cook for a further 2 minutes, or until heated through. Serve immediately, handing round the grated Parmesan cheese separately.

Cook's tip

White onions, which are very popular in Italy, are sweeter and milder than brown ones. Alternatively, you could use a red onion for this dish.

Vegetable Chilli

This is a hearty and flavoursome dish that works well served on its own, and is delicious spooned over cooked rice or baked potatoes to make a more substantial meal.

serves 4

1 aubergine, cut into 2.5-cm/1-inch slices

1 tbsp olive oil, plus extra for brushing

1 large red or yellow onion, finely chopped

2 red or yellow peppers, deseeded and finely chopped

3–4 garlic cloves, finely chopped or crushed

800 g/1 lb 12 oz canned chopped tomatoes

1 tbsp mild chilli powder

½ tsp ground cumin

½ tsp dried oregano

salt and pepper

2 small courgettes, quartered lengthways and sliced

400 g/14 oz canned kidney beans, drained and rinsed

450 ml/16 fl oz water

1 tbsp tomato purée

6 spring onions, finely chopped

115 g/4 oz Cheddar cheese, grated

Method

❶ Brush the aubergine slices on one side with oil. Heat half the oil in a frying pan. Add the slices, oiled-side up, and cook over a medium heat for 5–6 minutes, or until browned on one side. Turn the slices over and cook until browned. Transfer to a plate and cut into bite-sized pieces.

❷ Heat the remaining oil in a large saucepan over a medium heat. Add the chopped onion and peppers to the saucepan and cook, stirring occasionally, for 3–4 minutes, or until the onion is softened but not browned. Add the garlic and cook for a further 2–3 minutes, or until the onion begins to colour.

❸ Add the tomatoes, chilli powder, cumin and oregano to the saucepan, then season to taste. Bring just to the boil, reduce the heat, cover and simmer gently for 15 minutes.

❹ Add the courgettes, aubergine pieces and kidney beans. Stir in the water and tomato purée. Return to the boil, then cover the saucepan and simmer for a further 45 minutes, or until the vegetables are tender. Taste and adjust the seasoning, if necessary.

❺ Ladle into warmed bowls and top with spring onions and cheese.

Sweet & Sour Vegetables

This is a dish of Persian origin – not Chinese, as it sounds. Plump, diced aubergines are fried and mixed with tomatoes, mint, sugar and vinegar to give a unique combination of flavours.

serves 4

2 large aubergines

salt and pepper

6 tbsp olive oil

4 garlic cloves, crushed

1 onion, cut into eighths

4 large tomatoes, deseeded and chopped

3 tbsp chopped fresh mint

150 ml/5 fl oz vegetable stock

4 tsp brown sugar

2 tbsp red wine vinegar

1 tsp chilli flakes

fresh mint sprigs, to garnish

Method

❶ Cut the aubergines into cubes. Put them in a colander, sprinkle with plenty of salt and leave to stand for 30 minutes to remove all the bitter juices. Rinse thoroughly under cold running water and pat dry with kitchen paper.

❷ Heat the oil in a large, heavy-based frying pan. Add the aubergine and cook over a medium heat, stirring, for 1–2 minutes, or until beginning to colour. Stir in the garlic and onion wedges and cook, stirring constantly, for a further 2–3 minutes.

❸ Stir in the tomatoes, mint and stock. Reduce the heat, cover and simmer for 15–20 minutes, or until the aubergine and onion are tender.

❹ Add the brown sugar, red wine vinegar and chilli flakes, then season to taste and cook for a further 2–3 minutes, stirring.

❺ Transfer to a warmed serving dish, garnish with fresh mint sprigs and serve immediately.

Cook's tip

Choose firm, glossy aubergines for this dish. Large aubergines benefit from salting to extract their juices – small aubergines are less bitter, and can often be cooked without salting.

Yellow Curry

**Potatoes are not highly regarded in Thai cookery because rice is
the traditional staple food, but this dish is a tasty exception.**

serves 4

2 garlic cloves, finely chopped

3-cm/1¼-inch piece of galangal,
finely chopped

1 lemon grass stalk, finely chopped

1 tsp coriander seeds

3 tbsp vegetable oil

2 tsp Thai red curry paste

½ tsp ground turmeric

200 ml/7 fl oz coconut milk

250 g/9 oz potatoes, cut into cubes

100 ml/3½ fl oz vegetable stock

200 g/7 oz fresh young spinach leaves

1 small onion, thinly sliced into rings

Method

❶ Put the garlic, galangal, lemon grass
and coriander seeds into a mortar and
then crush with a pestle to make a
smooth paste.

❷ Heat 2 tablespoons of the oil in a large,
heavy-based frying pan or preheated wok.
Stir in the spice paste and the fresh garlic
and stir-fry over a high heat for
30 seconds. Stir in the curry paste and
turmeric, add the coconut milk and bring
to the boil.

❸ Add the potatoes and stock. Return to
the boil, then reduce the heat and simmer,
uncovered, for 10–12 minutes, or until the
potatoes are almost tender.

❹ Stir in the spinach and simmer until
the leaves have wilted.

❺ Heat the remaining oil in a separate
frying pan, add the onion and cook until
crisp and golden brown. Place on top of
the curry just before serving.

Cook's tip

*Choose a firm, waxy potato for this dish, one that
will keep its shape during cooking, in preference to
a floury variety that will break up easily.*

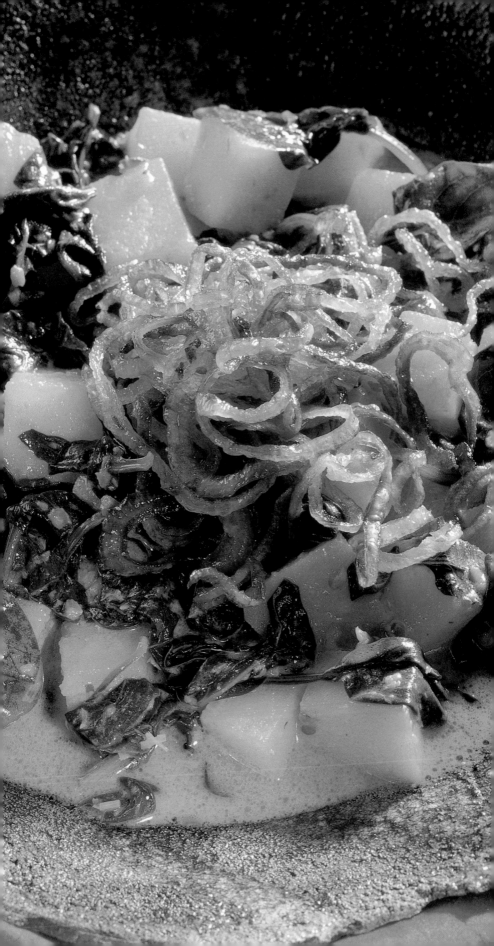

Greek Beans

This dish contains many typical Greek flavours, such as lemon and garlic, for a really flavoursome recipe. The fresh oregano and black olives give it a real taste of the Mediterranean.

serves 4

400 g/14 oz canned haricot beans, drained and rinsed

1 tbsp olive oil

3 garlic cloves, crushed

425 ml/15 fl oz vegetable stock

1 bay leaf

2 fresh oregano sprigs

1 tbsp tomato purée

juice of 1 lemon

1 small red onion, chopped

25 g/1 oz stoned black olives, halved

salt and pepper

Method

❶ Put the haricot beans into a flameproof casserole dish, add the oil and crushed garlic and cook over a low heat, stirring occasionally, for 4–5 minutes.

❷ Add the stock, bay leaf, oregano, tomato purée, lemon juice and red onion and stir to mix. Cover and simmer for 1 hour, or until the sauce has thickened.

❸ Stir in the black olives, then season the beans to taste. The dish is delicious served either warm or cold.

Cook's tip

You can substitute other canned beans for the haricot beans – try cannellini or black-eyed beans or chickpeas. Drain and rinse them before use – canned beans often have sugar or salt added.

Spiced Cashew Nut Curry

This unusual vegetarian dish is best served as a side dish with other curries and with rice to soak up the wonderfully rich, spiced juices.

serves 4

250 g/9 oz unsalted cashew nuts

1 small fresh green chilli

1 tsp coriander seeds

1 tsp cumin seeds

2 cardamom pods, crushed

1 tbsp sunflower oil

1 onion, thinly sliced

1 garlic clove, crushed

1 cinnamon stick

½ tsp ground turmeric

4 tbsp coconut cream

300 ml/10 fl oz hot vegetable stock

3 kaffir lime leaves, finely shredded

freshly cooked jasmine rice, to serve

Method

❶ Soak the cashew nuts in cold water for 8 hours, or overnight, then drain well. Deseed and chop the chilli. Put the coriander seeds, cumin seeds and cardamom pods into a mortar and crush with a pestle.

❷ Heat the oil in a heavy-based frying pan and stir-fry the onion and garlic over a medium heat for 2–3 minutes to soften, but not brown. Add the chilli, crushed spices, cinnamon stick and turmeric and stir-fry for a further 1 minute.

❸ Add the coconut cream and the hot stock to the frying pan. Bring to the boil, then add the cashew nuts and lime leaves. Reduce the heat, cover and simmer for 20 minutes. Serve hot, accompanied by freshly cooked jasmine rice.

Cook's tip

All spices give the best flavour when freshly crushed, but if you prefer, you can use ground spices instead of putting them into a mortar and crushing with a pestle.

Desserts

Creamed Rice Pudding

This rich, creamy rice dessert is a really comforting treat on cold winter days. You can serve it with a helping of canned or stewed fruit, or just enjoy it on its own.

serves 4

140 g/5 oz short-grain rice
1 litre/1¾ pints milk
115 g/4 oz sugar
1 tsp vanilla essence

To decorate
ground cinnamon
cinnamon sticks

Method

❶ Rinse the rice well under cold running water and drain. Pour the milk into a large, heavy-based saucepan, add the sugar and bring to the boil, stirring.

❷ Add the rice to the saucepan, then reduce the heat, cover and simmer gently, stirring occasionally, for 1 hour, or until the milk has been absorbed.

❸ Stir in the vanilla essence. Transfer to tall heatproof glasses, lightly dust with ground cinnamon and serve immediately, decorated with cinnamon sticks.

Variation

For an orange flavour, omit the sugar and vanilla and stir 3 tablespoons of clear honey and the finely grated rind of 1 orange into the milk in Step 1.

Teacup Pudding

This is such an easy dessert to make, because all the ingredients, except the mixed spice, can be measured in the same cup. It tastes best served with a generous helping of warmed custard.

serves 4

butter, for greasing

1 cup self-raising flour

1 tsp mixed spice

1 cup soft brown sugar

1 cup shredded suet

1 cup currants

1 cup milk

custard, to serve

Method

❶ Grease a 1-litre/1¾-pint pudding basin with butter. Sift the flour and mixed spice into a mixing bowl and stir in the sugar, suet and currants, then add the milk and mix well. Spoon the mixture into the prepared basin.

❷ Cut out a circle of greaseproof paper and a circle of foil 7.5 cm/3 inches larger than the rim of the pudding basin. Place the paper circle on top of the foil circle, grease it, and pleat both circles across the centre. Place them over the basin, paper-side down, and tie around the rim with string.

❸ Place the pudding basin on a trivet in a large saucepan and fill with boiling water to come halfway up the sides. Alternatively, place it in a steamer over a saucepan of boiling water. Steam for 3 hours, then carefully remove from the saucepan. Discard the covering, turn out on to a warmed serving dish and serve with custard.

Cook's tip

It doesn't matter whether you use a standard measuring cup (225 ml/8 fl oz) or an ordinary teacup to measure the ingredients, because the proportions remain the same.

Clafoutis

Although the many different recipes for this unusual, batter-based dessert may use a variety of fruits, cherries are the classic filling in Limousin in France, where the dish originated.

serves 4

450 g/1 lb sweet black cherries

2 tbsp cherry brandy

1 tbsp icing sugar, plus extra
for dusting

butter, for greasing

Batter

3 tbsp plain flour

3 tbsp sugar

175 ml/6 fl oz single cream

2 eggs, lightly beaten

grated rind of ½ lemon

¼ tsp vanilla essence

Method

❶ Preheat the oven to 190°C/375°F/ Gas Mark 5. Stone the cherries, then place in a bowl with the cherry brandy and icing sugar and mix together. Cover with clingfilm and leave to stand for 1 hour.

❷ Meanwhile, grease a shallow, ovenproof dish with butter. To make the batter, sift the flour into a bowl and stir in the sugar. Gradually whisk in the single cream, beaten eggs, lemon rind and vanilla essence. Whisk constantly until the batter is completely smooth.

❸ Spoon the cherries into the ovenproof dish and pour the batter over them to cover. Bake in the preheated oven for 45 minutes, or until golden and set. Lightly dust with extra icing sugar and serve warm, or leave to cool to room temperature before serving.

Cook's tip

Traditionally, in Limousin, the cherries are not stoned before cooking, because the stones are thought to release extra flavour into the dessert.

Tarte Tatin

This upside-down apple tart has been a speciality of Sologne in the Loire valley for centuries, but was made famous by the Tatin sisters who ran a hotel-restaurant in Lamotte-Beuvron at the beginning of the twentieth century.

serves 8

225 g/8 oz shortcrust pastry, thawed if frozen

plain flour, for dusting

10 eating apples, such as Golden Delicious

4 tbsp lemon juice

115 g/4 oz unsalted butter, diced

115 g/4 oz caster sugar

½ tsp ground cinnamon

Method

❶ Preheat the oven to 230°C/450°F/ Gas Mark 8. Roll out the pastry on a lightly floured work surface into a 5-mm/¼-inch thick round, about 28 cm/ 11 inches in diameter. Transfer to a lightly floured baking tray and leave to chill in the refrigerator.

❷ Peel, halve and core the apples, then brush with the lemon juice to prevent any discoloration. Heat the butter, sugar and cinnamon in a 25-cm/10-inch tarte tatin tin or heavy-based frying pan with a flameproof handle over a low heat, stirring occasionally, until the butter has melted and the sugar has dissolved. Cook for a further 6–8 minutes, or until the mixture is a light caramel colour. Remove from the heat.

❸ Arrange the apples in the tin or frying pan, packing them in tightly. Return to the heat and cook for 25 minutes, or until the apples are tender and lightly coloured. Remove from the heat and leave to cool slightly.

❹ Place the pastry over the apples, tucking in the edges. Prick the top and bake in the preheated oven for 30 minutes, or until golden. Leave to cool slightly, then run a knife around the edge of the tin to loosen the pastry. Invert on to a plate and serve warm.

Cook's tip

To achieve the best decorative effect when the tart is turned over, pack the halved apples in the tin with their cut sides facing up in Step 3.

Flambéed Peaches

This dessert is a fabulous end to a dinner party – especially if your guests are watching you cook. It makes a luxurious but, at the same time, refreshing final course.

serves 4

3 tbsp unsalted butter

3 tbsp muscovado sugar

4 tbsp orange juice

4 peaches, peeled, halved and stoned

2 tbsp almond liqueur or peach brandy

4 tbsp toasted flaked almonds

Method

❶ Heat the butter, muscovado sugar and orange juice in a large, heavy-based frying pan over a low heat, stirring constantly, until the butter has melted and the sugar has dissolved.

❷ Add the peaches and cook for 1–2 minutes on each side, or until golden.

❸ Add the almond liqueur and ignite with a match or taper. When the flames have died down, transfer to serving dishes, sprinkle with toasted flaked almonds and serve immediately.

Cook's tip

Igniting the spirit will burn off the alcohol and mellow the flavour. However, if you are serving this dessert to children, you can omit the almond liqueur or brandy.

Apple Fritters

This is a very popular choice for family meals, as children and adults alike love the flavour and crispy texture of the apple rings – and you don't need a spoon or fork to eat them.

serves 4

115 g/4 oz plain flour

pinch of salt

2 egg yolks

1 egg white

1 tbsp sunflower oil

150 ml/5 fl oz milk

450 g/1 lb cooking apples

juice of 1 lemon

caster sugar, for sprinkling

115 g/4 oz unsalted butter

crème fraîche, to serve

Method

❶ Sift the flour and salt into a mixing bowl. Make a well in the centre and add the egg yolks, egg white and oil. Gradually incorporate the flour into the liquid with a wooden spoon. Gradually beat in the milk and continue beating to make a smooth batter. Cover with clingfilm and leave to stand for 30 minutes.

❷ Peel and core the apples, then cut them into rings about 5-mm/¼-inch thick. Spread them out on a plate and then sprinkle with the lemon juice and caster sugar.

❸ Melt the butter in a large, heavy-based frying pan over a medium heat. Dip the apple rings into the batter, one at a time, then drop them into the frying pan. Cook for 2–3 minutes on each side, or until golden. Transfer to a serving platter, sprinkle with more caster sugar and serve with crème fraîche.

Cook's tip

Choose firm, tart apples for this dish, such as Bramleys or Granny Smiths. Once they are cut, they should be sprinkled with lemon juice immediately and cooked quickly to prevent any discoloration.

Syllabub

Wine, brandy and cream make this old-fashioned dessert wonderfully self-indulgent – and it is guaranteed to make an impression if you serve it at a dinner party.

serves 6

175 ml/6 fl oz Madeira
2 tbsp brandy
grated rind of 1 lemon
125 ml/4 fl oz lemon juice
115 g/4 oz caster sugar

600 ml/1 pint double cream
10 amaretti biscuits or
ratafias, crumbled
ground cinnamon, to dust
lemon slices, to decorate

Method

❶ Whisk the Madeira, brandy, lemon rind, lemon juice and caster sugar in a bowl until combined.

❷ Add the cream to the bowl and continue whisking until the mixture is thick in consistency.

❸ Divide the biscuits between 6 long-stemmed glasses or sundae dishes. Fill each glass or dish with the syllabub mixture and leave in the refrigerator to chill until ready to serve, if desired. Dust the surface of each dessert with ground cinnamon and decorate with lemon slices, and serve.

Cook's tip

Madeira is a fortified wine from the island of the same name. It may be dry, medium or sweet. Dessert Madeira is best for this recipe – use Bual or Malmsey.

Zabaglione

This light and frothy, warm dessert, which originates from Italy, is a welcome treat at the end of a meal. You should serve zabaglione as soon as it is ready, to appreciate its full flavour.

serves 6

4 egg yolks

70 g/2½ oz caster sugar

125 ml/4 fl oz Marsala wine

amaretti biscuits, to serve

Method

❶ Half fill a saucepan with water and bring to the boil. Reduce the heat so that the water is barely simmering. Beat the egg yolks and sugar in a heatproof bowl with an electric whisk until pale and creamy.

❷ Set the bowl over the saucepan of water. Do not let the base touch the surface of the water, or the egg yolks will scramble.

❸ Gradually add the Marsala wine, beating constantly with the electric whisk. Continue beating until the mixture is thick and has increased in volume. Pour into heatproof glasses or bowls and serve immediately with amaretti biscuits.

Cook's tip

Decorate the zabaglione with a slit strawberry, placed on the rim of the glass, or serve with sponge fingers or crisp biscuits.

Recipe List

- Apple Fritters *90* • Bacon & Lentil Soup *12* • Beef & Vegetable Soup *14*

- Beef in Beer with Herb Dumplings *18* • Beef Stroganoff *16* • Boston Fish Pie *52*

- Brunswick Stew *32* • Cauliflower Bake *58* • Chicken Pasanda *36* • Clafoutis *84*

- Cock-a-Leekie *10* • Coq au Vin *38* • Creamed Rice Pudding *80*

- Flambéed Peaches *88* • French Country Casserole *26* • Greek Beans *74*

- Irish Stew *22* • Italian Turkey Steaks *42* • Jambalaya *34* • Mexican Turkey *40*

- Moroccan Lamb *24* • Moules Marinières *50* • Paella del Mar *48* • Paprika Pork *28*

- Pepper & Mushroom Hash *60* • Pot-roast Pork *30* • Potato-topped Vegetables *64*

- Risotto Primavera *66* • Seafood Risotto *44* • Spiced Cashew Nut Curry *76*

- Stifado *20* • Sweet & Sour Vegetables *70* • Sweetcorn, Potato & Cheese Soup *56*

- Syllabub *92* • Tarte Tatin *86* • Teacup Pudding *82* • Thai Prawn Curry *46*

- Vegetable Chilli *68* • Winter Cobbler *62* • Yellow Curry *72* • Zabaglione *94*